MAKING PEACE WITH YOUR EMOTIONS

MAKING PEACE WITH YOUR EMOTIONS

LIVING LIFE TO THE FULLEST

Margaret Feinberg

Foreword by Marilyn Meberg

THOMAS NELSON
Since 1798

NASHVILLE DALLAS MEXICO CITY RIO DE JANEIRO

Published in Nashville, Tennessee, by Thomas Nelson. Thomas Nelson is a trademark of Thomas Nelson, Inc.

Thomas Nelson, Inc., titles may be purchased in bulk for educational, business, fund-raising, or sales promotional use. For information, please e-mail SpecialMarkets@ThomasNelson.com.

Library of Congress Cataloging-in-Publication

ISBN: 978-1-4185-4930-5

Printed in China

11 12 13 14 RRD 5 4 3 2 1

Contents

Foreword

Who does not want to "make peace" with their emotions? There are times when we are at peace with our emotions; they please us. We don't feel at war with them. They bring us happiness, contentedness, and at times, huge hoots of laughter. We can feel the quiet peace produced by God's incomparable scenic beauty or the sheer exuberance of a perfect chocolate desert. We recognize that without our emotions, life would feel flat, gray, or dead. We need our emotions to remind us we are alive.

But our lively emotions can erupt into expressions of fury and nearly murderous anger. We are horrified to realize the depth of those feelings and fear the possibilities of the behavior that fury might produce. We do our best to hide the feelings from others and even from ourselves. We pretend we are fine and slap on a fake smile and hope nothing leaks out from behind it. In spite of our efforts to camouflage, our anger causes us to feel nervous about ourselves. We realize anger's internal and continual perking operates much like an old coffee maker with no automatic shut-off switch.

In addition to feeling fearful about our anger's potential to do harm, we also feel shame. Those shame feelings have a voice. They say: *What is wrong with you? You should not have those feelings of rage. You're a Christian . . . at least you claim to be. Maybe you really are not a Christian; maybe you are a fake. No one who is a true Christian has those thoughts and feelings. You should just quit pretending to be someone you are not*. It's at this point that we recognize the need to somehow make peace with these emotions. But how?

Jealousy is another lively emotion that can either erupt unexpectedly or, like anger, perk away beneath our well-guarded exterior. We may be uncomfortably aware of the Galatians 5:26 warning that we "not become conceited, provoking one another, envying one another." That admonition could not be clearer. Our struggle could not be more difficult.

What causes us to want, crave, plot, or even fake what does not belong to us? We know the bottom-line answer to that question is we crave and fake because our hearts are incurably wicked (Jeremiah 17:9). But we ask the age-old question, "Shouldn't I who knows 'the cure' behave better?" Not sure how to answer ourselves, we, yet again climb on the shame treadmill and walk it until we're exhausted. So I'll say it again: it is at this point that we recognize the need to make peace with these emotions. But how?

I love it when the "but how" questions in life have an answer. Margaret Feinberg's *Making Peace with Your Emotions: Living Life to the Fullest* is filled with scriptural ways we can truly make peace with the emotions that shame us and rob us of ever feeling there is truly a way to "live life to the fullest." With the expertise of Margaret's biblical insights and empathic suggestions, you will find yourself discovering reasons for hope to change what you once found hopeless and beyond changing.

It is always reassuring to remember that God cares even more than we do about our unruly emotions. In fact, He created those emotions. Not only did He create our emotions, He feels them Himself.

You are going to find that this study is meant just for you. Your emotions can be wonderfully enriching friends. I suggest you prepare to have a whole new appreciation for them. In fact, you may learn to love yourself like Jesus loves you!

—Marilyn Meberg

Introduction

Delighting in Your Emotions

To give up enthusiasm wrinkles the soul.

Samuel Ullman,
American poet

What would it be like to live in a world void of vibrant colors? Imagine for a moment that everything was black, white, and matte grey. The sky. The trees. The animals. Not just everyone around you, but even you. Without color, we'd miss out on the royal blues and purples that paint the sky as the sun melts into the horizon. We'd never experience the fluorescent shades of tropical birds or fish. The beauty of spring blossoms would be muted. Life would lose its vibrancy, the delight that comes with its diverse and beautiful expressions. Such a scene makes us grateful for all the hues that God has given us.

Now imagine for a moment a world void of emotion. Like a world without color, one without emotion would lack the delight and wonder that God intends. Without emotion, we couldn't experience the delicate joy of holding a newborn baby in our arms. Apart from emotion, we wouldn't savor the comfort of a tender embrace.

Without emotions, we couldn't respond in awe to a surprise given to us by those who love and know us best.

Indeed, one of the greatest gifts God has given us is our emotions. It's no accident that God gives us the ability to feel a wide range of feelings from anticipation to joy. Just as color gives our world brightness and beauty, emotions give our lives feelings and unforgettable experiences.

While you may be tempted to list a few emotions you wish you didn't have such as anger or sadness, even those feelings are divine gifts meant to be celebrated. Why? Because God feels them too! Those emotions provide a glimpse into God's heart, and it isn't a mistake that you experience them.

Throughout this study, we'll look at a handful of the emotions you've probably felt. These are emotions people have been experiencing since the beginning of time. We'll examine the idea that not only did God create us and give us emotions, but He feels them Himself too. And we'll look at emotions that are truly a gift—whether it's fear or anger or joy—and unpack their holy dimensions.

My hope and prayer is that throughout this study, you'll find yourself delighting in the emotions that God has given you. And along the way you'll find yourself coming alive in the fullness of all God has called and created you to be.

Blessings,
Margaret Feinberg

Emotions Are God's Gift

While we may convince ourselves that we don't really need emotions or that somehow emotions can get in our way, God created us with emotions. We were designed to experience feelings. The good news is that not only did God create emotions as a gift, but He feels them Himself too.

One

Rejoice! And Again I Say Rejoice!

Over and over [the Psalms] attest to the reality that when we open our minds and hearts fully to the God who made them, then we open ourselves, whether we know it or not, to the possibility of being transformed beyond our imagining.

Ellen F. Davis,
theologian and author

Everyone is created with a different kind of emotional makeup. Some people wear their emotions on their sleeve, while others are more reserved. Some people display a wide range of emotions; others experience a more narrow range of feelings; and some people can identify not only what they're feeling, but what everyone else in the room is feeling as well. Take the following Emotional Response Quiz to learn more about how you experience and express emotions.

Emotional Response Quiz

1. *You receive an email letting you know that one of your friends has just lost her job. Your first reaction is to:*

   a. *Consider the reasons she may have lost her job, reflect on the financial challenges she'll face as a result, and think about possible solutions to help her find another job as soon as possible.*

   b. *Reach for a tissue, because you know how much this job meant to your friend and the financial blow the loss of work will create for her. You can almost feel the stress and tension that she must be feeling. Rather than pick up the phone, you hop in the car to drive to her house to offer empathy and support.*

   c. *Decide the best course of action is to write a quick email response that you're praying for her through this time.*

2. *You are driving to the grocery store and stop at a red light when you feel the vehicle behind you bump into your car. You get out of the vehicle to inspect the damage and discover a gash in the bumper of your car. You respond by:*

   a. *Talking to the driver to assess what caused the accident. Then you look around to see who might have witnessed the accident. You carefully decide whether or not the accident warrants a police report and proceed accordingly.*

   b. *Taking a gulp and pushing back the tears. Though you tell yourself it's just a car, you can't help but feel the impact of the moment. This accident was the last thing you needed today, and you don't want to let it push you over the edge. But looking in the eyes of the other driver, you can't help but feel compassion. This was probably the last thing he needed today too.*

c. Looking at your watch and wondering how long the accident will delay you from getting to your next appointment. You exchange information with the other driver, and leave the scene of the accident knowing that the event was more of an inconvenience than anything else.

3. *You step on the scale and discover you've put on more weight than you'd hoped after the holidays. You respond by:*

   a. Developing a detailed eating and exercise plan to lose the weight in the next thirty days.

   b. Fighting back the tears at the thought of having to go on a diet and enroll in a weight-loss program.

   c. Recognizing that you need to make better decisions in eating and exercise and mentally commit to doing so.

4. *You receive news that you're receiving a bonus at work. You respond by:*

   a. Carefully calculating the best way to spend and invest the money.

   b. Sitting down at your desk and emailing everyone who you think it's appropriate to tell the good news. For the rest of the day, you feel like you're walking on cloud nine.

   c. Expressing gratitude to your boss and sharing the news with your family and friends when you get home that day.

Scoring

Add up the total number of A's, B's, and C's that you scored.

If you answered mostly A's, you tend to have a Thinking Response. When you're confronted with challenges in life, you prefer to look for solutions. You've probably made more than one pros-versus-cons list in your life as you've weighed a decision. At times, you're slower to respond to a situation because of the entire

evaluation taking place in your mind. While you feel emotions, you recognize the importance of rational thought and keeping a clear head in tough situations.

If you answered mostly B's, you tend to have an Emotional Response. When you're confronted with challenges in life, you tend to feel a response in yourself and empathize with the responses of others. This makes you sensitive and compassionate as well as quick to serve. Sometimes you may be tempted to share too much of what you're feeling, but when you share appropriately you can help people get in touch with what they're feeling and experiencing inside.

God gave you an emotional makeup and wants to use you as an instrument to share the love of God with others and bring glory to Himself.

If you answered mostly C's, you tend to have a Reserved Response. When you're confronted with challenges in life, you both think and feel, but those around you may only notice your stability and dependability in the moment. At times you may struggle to express your emotions, which makes it difficult for others to know what you're feeling, but you come off as even-keeled, a rock. As a result people feel safe expressing their own feelings around you.

While you may be tempted to think, *I wish I was more like so-and-so* in your emotional responses, the truth is that you are carefully and wonderfully made. God gave you an emotional makeup and wants to use you—just as you are—as an instrument to share the love of God with others and bring glory to Himself. He made us all unique, and we need each other—sometimes to have a Thinking Response, sometimes to have an Emotional Response, and sometimes to have a Reserved Response as we journey through life together as the children of God.

1. *What did the Emotional Responder Quiz reveal about how you tend to respond to situations? Have you always responded primarily in this way, or can you identify a time in your life when you used to respond differently?*

mostly C's Reserved Response
always been that way.
nickname - "calm Connie"

2. *What are some of the strengths about the way you respond emotionally to challenges in life? What are some of the weaknesses about the way you respond emotionally to challenges in life?*

I sometimes think I miss
how others are feeling &
am not as empathetic as
I could be.

When it comes to our emotions, we may be tempted to hide what we're feeling from God, but the Psalms are a powerful reminder that God invites us to be honest with Him about what we're thinking, feeling, and experiencing in our lives. They invite us to fully disclose ourselves to God.

3. *Read* **Psalm 6.** *Make a list of emotions that David expressed to God in this psalm.*

faint
deep anguish
worn out
tearful
sorrow

Known as one of the lament psalms, Psalm 6 expresses a wide range of emotions to God, and if you look at the passage closely, you'll notice the transformation that takes place in David's heart. He begins at a low point of brokenness and pain but ends with the hope that not only has God heard his prayer, but his enemies will be put to shame. David begins with one perspective but ends with a completely different one.

4. *When in the last three months have you found that your perspective changed when you fully expressed yourself to God?*

worried about children, but realized I have to put them in God's hands.

5. *When you're tempted to have an overly emotional or cerebral response to a situation or person, who do you usually unleash your emotions or thoughts on? What is the result?*

spouse, children sister, close friend

6. *What benefits do you think can be found in expressing your emotions to God first?*

He can help us see a different perspective.

The book of Psalms contains 150 psalms that were written by many anonymous poets and musicians. Psalms, which were actually songs, had many different purposes. Of all the different types of psalms, the psalms of lament are the most numerous, often asking the tough question of "Why?" and expressing a wide range of emotions. Yet the lament psalms often end by placing trust and faith in God. Not only has the psalmist been heard, but the writings end in the hope that God will answer.

Some psalms were used in worship services as a type of liturgy (Psalms 2 and 50). Some expressed thanksgiving or praise (Psalms 18; 107; 138), while others celebrated the saving actions of God from the past and celebrated the promises and faithfulness of God (Psalm 131).

7. *Read* **Psalm 30**. *As what type of psalm would you classify this passage? When in your own life have you been in a situation in which you could identify with the emotions expressed in this psalm?*

thanksgiving + praise

8. *What holds you back from fully disclosing your thoughts and feelings to God in prayer? How do the Psalms encourage you that you can express anything to God?*

Thinking I can handle things myself.

The Psalms are a powerful reminder that we can bring ourselves, our whole selves including our emotions, before God and discover God's loving care no matter what we're facing.

Digging Deeper

Read Psalm 1. How have you found the principles expressed in this passage to be true in your own life? Why is it important to reflect and meditate on passages of Scripture like this one? How does reading the Psalms affect your attitude and perspective on the challenges you're facing in life? Praying the Psalms is great when you don't know what to pray.

Bonus Activity

Spend a few moments prayerfully reflecting on the challenges and the joys that you're facing in life right now. Compose your own psalm to God. The piece can be as short or as long as you'd like. Use your own words to prayerfully express what's going on in your heart and life right now.

Two

Spiritual Awakenings

Faith, mighty faith, the promise sees,
And looks to God alone; Laughs at
impossibilities, And cries it shall be done.

CHARLES WESLEY,
BRITISH POET

The story of John Wesley, the founder of the Methodist church, having his heart strangely warmed in an encounter with God is well-known in many circles. But lesser known is the story of younger brother, Charles, who helped form the denomination alongside him.

In 1738, Charles was suffering from pneumonia and wasn't expected to survive. Lying on his deathbed, the thirty-year-old slipped in and out of consciousness. Hot flashes and cold spells chilled his weakening body.

On the day of Pentecost, Charles awoke to see a family friend, Mrs. Musgrave, at the side of his bed. She gently said, "In the name of Jesus of Nazareth, I tell you, arise and believe, and you shall be healed of your infirmities." Charles wanted to respond, but too weak to answer, he watched in silence as she slipped out of the room.

Charles suddenly felt a "strange palpitation" in his heart. Energy returned to his body. The signs of pneumonia began to fade. He was regaining his health, but not just his physical health. Something else was beginning to happen. Though Charles had grown up in an Anglican home and become a priest, he still longed for the deeper assurance of faith that he'd seen in other Christians. For the first time in his life, the younger Wesley brother felt a solid assurance of his salvation. "I believe," he announced. "I do believe."

For the first time in his life, the younger Wesley brother felt a solid assurance of his salvation.

After his recovery, Charles saw Mrs. Musgrave and asked what compelled her to visit him and speak those words. At first she denied the encounter, but later admitted she was simply obeying what Christ had commanded her.

Three days later, John Wesley had an encounter with God in which his heart was strangely warmed.

From that day forward, Charles celebrated Pentecost with a profound spiritual fervor. The holiday was more than a liturgical observance in the Christian calendar; it became the day Charles celebrated becoming a committed follower of Christ who was guided by the Holy Spirit. He went on to pen dozens of hymns celebrating the day of Pentecost and encouraging others, including his own brother, to encounter the fullness of God.

On October 28, 1762, Charles's older brother, John, wrote: *"Many years ago my brother frequently said, 'Your day of Pentecost is not fully come; but I doubt not it will; and you will then hear of persons sanctified as frequently as you do now of persons justified.' Any unprejudiced reader may observe that it was now fully come."*[1]

Charles continued to remind his brother and anyone who would listen of the importance of the "Days of Pentecost," personal and community-wide spiritual awakenings in which people become more intimate followers of Jesus, experiencing the joys of His presence and faithfulness in their lives.

God used a spiritual awakening in the lives of Charles and John Wesley in order to touch their lives and empower them. For both men, the experiences affected not just their minds but their hearts. The divine encounters touched their emotions. In our own spiritual journeys, sometimes God will touch our emotions in unexpected ways and use the experiences to profoundly shape our lives.

1. *Like Charles and John Wesley, when in your own life have you experienced a spiritual "aha" moment when the lights came on and you discovered something new about God, others, or yourself? How did the experience change you?*

2. *How would you define the term "spiritual awakening" in your own life? Do you think it's possible to have a spiritual awakening in your life without having your emotions affected? Why or why not?*

The idea of experiencing a spiritual awakening or having one's heart strangely warmed might seem strange, until we remember that this is the very thing Jesus came to do. Time and time again throughout the Gospels, Jesus opened people's eyes and hearts to the reality of God—most unexpectedly, He did this after His resurrection.

3. *Take turns reading* **Luke 24:13–35**. *What do you think the two men were thinking and feeling as they travelled and talked?*

sadness, anger

4. *How would you evaluate the beliefs of the two men as they explained their understanding of Jesus (hint: vv. 19–24)?*

They had hoped Jesus was the Messiah. Now they weren't so sure

5. *Why did Jesus rebuke the two walking on the road to Emmaus (hint: vv. 25–26)? Do you think Jesus' rebuke was warranted? Why or why not? In what ways are Jesus' words to the men true in your life right now?*

They had not realized how Christ had fulfilled prophecy.

At one point in their journey, Jesus acted as if He would travel farther without the two men (v. 28). The moment was a small test to see if the men really wanted to continue the conversation with Jesus.

6. *How did the men respond to Jesus acting as if He was going to travel on without them (hint: v. 29)? What does it look like for you in your own spiritual life to urge God to stay with you?*

They urged Him to stay with them.

7. *Make a list of the emotions the two men may have felt as their hearts burned within them.*

They were drinking in all the knowledge & insight Jesus had.

8. *When have you experienced your heart burning within you as the Scriptures were opened to you? What passages from Scripture have been the most meaningful to you to fan the flame of faith in your life?*

Psalms

Spiritual awakenings in our lives rarely happen apart from our emotions. Most often when we encounter God we'll feel a sense of the joy, delight, confidence, or hope that comes from knowing God more intimately.

Digging Deeper

Being a prophet isn't always easy. Just ask Jeremiah. This Old Testament prophet complained about the frustrations of having to relay messages that weren't always good news. Read **Jeremiah 20:7–18.** How did Jeremiah describe what it was like to hold back and not speak as a prophet (v. 9)? Why was it important for Jeremiah to deliver the word of the Lord? When have you sensed a conviction to say something? How did you respond to the situation? In what ways can you empathize with Jeremiah's struggles?

Bonus Activity

Make a list of five scriptures that have been most meaningful to you in your life. Spend some time prayerfully reflecting on what those passages have in common. Thank God for the ways He has been true to the words of those passages in various ages and stages in your life.

Claudette's mom - Nancy Cadwell

Three

The Wonder of Divine Emotions

God has not created man to be a stock or stone but has given him five senses and a heart of flesh, so that he loves his friends, is angry with his enemies, and commiserates with his dear friends in adversity.

MARTIN LUTHER,
PROTESTANT THEOLOGIAN

Jesus felt many different emotions throughout His life. Imagine the emotions Jesus experienced when He said to some of the first disciples, "Follow Me," and they left everything they had to walk with Him. Or at the wedding in Cana when Jesus' mother persisted over an issue that wasn't His concern, namely, the wedding party had run out of wine. Or the moment Jesus saw the woman at the well and refused to look away. Or the healing of a man who had been unable to walk his entire life but then took his first steps. Or the delight he saw in a young boy's face as a humble lunch offering become a feast for thousands. Or the frustration Jesus felt toward religious leaders who, despite knowing the Hebrew Scriptures backward and forward, refused to believe.

The gospel of John describes Jesus as "the Word became flesh and dwelt among us" (1:14). The mystery and wonder of this proclamation is that Jesus became God incarnate—both fully divine and fully human—and felt a wide range of emotions.

Jesus wore His emotions on His sleeve, revealing His heart for the people.

One of Jesus' most emotional displays is tucked into John 11 when He received the news that Lazarus, His dear friend and the brother of Mary and Martha, was sick. Verse 5 reveals how Jesus felt about this family: He loved them. Yet rather than respond to the urgent news, Jesus remained where He was for two additional days knowing that Lazarus's death would be transformed into a profound moment of glorifying God.

When Jesus arrived, Lazarus had already died. Martha ran to meet Jesus arguing that if only He had been present, her brother would not have died. Meanwhile, Mary sat in her home mourning the loss. Upon Jesus' arrival, Mary offered the same argument as her sister verbatim. When Jesus saw everyone around Him weeping, "He groaned in the spirit and was troubled" (v. 33).

Then we find the shortest verse in most versions of the Bible: "Jesus wept" (v. 35). Jesus wore His emotions on His sleeve, revealing His heart for the people.

Then Jesus followed the family to the tomb and instructed them to remove the stone. Martha protested, but Jesus challenged her and said the glory of God was about to be displayed. Jesus prayed and then issued the command, "Lazarus, come forth!" (v. 43).

A dead man, wrapped in cloth, emerged from the tomb. Mary and Martha received their brother back, and God was glorified as many came to believe in Jesus.

One of the extraordinary aspects of this story is that Jesus already knew the miracle that was going to take place, yet chose to feel empathy and mourn with those who were mourning. The hot tears that rolled down Jesus' cheeks were an outward sign that He felt their pain and loss.

Jesus entered our world not only physically but emotionally. This is good news because it means there isn't an emotion that we encounter that's foreign to God. Not only did God create emotions, but He experiences them as well, which gives us encouragement that no matter what we're feeling, God knows and understands. Whether we cry out to Him in joy or tears, God responds with compassion and love as one who is Emmanuel—God with us.

1. *Take turns reading* **John 11**. *What details of this story are most interesting to you? Why?*

2. *What does this story and Jesus' emotional response reveal about His relationship with Martha, Mary, and Lazarus? What does the timing of Lazarus's death (v. 17) reveal about where Jesus was staying when the message arrived (v. 6)?*

Jesus' life and His emotions are highlighted throughout all of the Gospels. The gospel of Luke in particular highlights several of Jesus' emotional encounters.

3. *Read* **Luke 7:1–10**. *What emotion(s) did Jesus display in this passage? What was the outcome of Jesus' response to the centurion? In the past seven days, when have you felt this emotion in your own life? How did you respond?* amazement

4. *Read* **Luke 7:11–17**. *What emotion(s) did Jesus display in this passage? What was the outcome of Jesus' response to the woman? In the past seven days, when have you felt this emotion in your own life? How did you respond?* compassion, pity

5. *Read* **Luke 8:22–25**. *What emotion(s) did Jesus display in this passage? What was the outcome of Jesus' response to the storm? In the past seven days, when have you felt this emotion in your own life? How did you respond?* sternness?
impatience?

6. *Read* **Luke 10:17–22**. *What emotion(s) did Jesus display in this passage? What was the outcome of Jesus' response to the news of the seventy? In the past seven days, when have you felt this emotion in your own life? How did you respond?* full of joy through the H.S.

7. *In your own life, when do your emotions most reflect the attitude, actions, and activities of Jesus?*

8. *When do your emotions prevent you from reflecting the attitude, actions, and activities of Jesus? What makes the difference between your emotions reflecting or not reflecting Christ?*

> *Jesus displayed a wide range of emotions, and so do we. There is freedom in allowing ourselves to process those emotions. The challenge comes in handling our emotions in ways that reflect His work in our lives.*

Digging Deeper

Luke 15 records multiple parables in which Jesus expressed His compassion for the lost. Read **Luke 15:1–10.** Reflecting on this passage, what is the emotional response to finding that which was lost? Imagine yourself as the shepherd and woman. What emotions would you feel upon rediscovering that which was lost? How often in your own life do you rejoice and celebrate with others who are discovering God and His presence in their life? What prevents you from celebrating more often?

Bonus Activity

Prayerfully ask God to reveal one person whom you can rejoice with over the course of the next week. A birthday. A new birth. A job promotion. An announcement of good news. Go out of your way to celebrate with the person and share the joy God has given you with them.

Emotions You Can't Live Without

Sometimes we may be tempted to look at an emotion and think, **I wish I never felt that**! *But all the emotions God gives us are meant for good. We simply need to make sure that we express our emotions in healthy ways that bring glory to God.*

Four

Fear Not! Well, Maybe a Little!

Each time we face our fear, we gain strength, courage, and confidence in the doing.

UNKNOWN

An old Aesop fable tells the story of a mouse that lived in the house of a famous magician. Nearly every day the magician watched the small creature cower in shadows and dart between furniture in terror of a large but lazy cat who was blind in one eye. Taking pity on the mouse, the magician decided to turn the mouse into a cat.

The mouse was thrilled with his new body until he realized that the magician also owned a dog that wasn't as lazy or blind as the previous cat. Paralyzed by fear, the animal stood on the top of a couch and refused to move. The fear of the dog was simply too much.

Again, the magician had compassion and transformed the mouse-turned-cat into a dog. But even as a dog, the creature realized there was something to be scared of, namely, the tiger the magician kept in his home and used for his performances.

Looking at the cowering animal, the magician said, "Be a mouse again. As you have only the heart of a mouse, it is impossible to help you by giving you the body of a noble animal."

The story illustrates that when we become gripped by fear it affects our entire being. The mouse could not rid himself of his fear—despite his change in form. No matter what the magician tried, he could not take away the fear that overtook the mouse's heart and mind. The timid mouse allowed fear to paralyze him.

An unhealthy dose of fear in our lives has paralyzing results. Unhealthy fear can result in removing ourselves from relationships, activities, and events that would not only give us life but allow us to share the life of God with others.

A healthy dose of fear is a God-given gift.

Now, it's important to remember that not all fear is bad. Sometimes we can look at an emotion and wish that it would go away, not realizing that God has given us that very emotion to help protect and guard us. But a healthy dose of fear is a God-given gift.

Healthy fear reminds us to stay away from dangerous situations. The acknowledgment that something bad might happen challenges us to make good choices. Drive the speed limit. Wear a seat belt. Check in the rearview mirror before changing lanes. Look both ways before crossing the street. Healthy fear keeps us safe.

While we aren't meant to live in fear, a healthy dose of fear helps keep us safe, allows us to walk in wisdom, and provides an appropriate understanding of our limitations.

1. *What surprises you about the story of the scared mouse? In what ways do you relate to this story?*

always look greener on the other side!

2. *What are your top five fears? Which of the fears listed affect your life most on a daily basis?*

fear of loss of family member
getting up in front of people
fear of end time events

Not only is fear challenging for us, but even Jesus' disciples experienced and expressed fear. Peter, the disciple whom Jesus promised to build His church upon, displayed fear that reflected his lack of faith in Christ.

3. *Take turns reading* **Matthew 14:22–33**. *What were the disciples fearful of first (hint: v. 26)? What was Jesus' response? When was the last time you found yourself in a situation that made you feel like the disciples did?*

They thought Christ was a ghost.
"Come"

Peter boldly told Jesus to command him to walk on the water. Jesus called to Peter to get out of the boat. Sometimes Jesus issues a similar call to us by inviting us to step out of the boat and do something we think is impossible.

4. *What was Peter's fear in Matthew 14:30? What was Jesus' response to Peter's sinking? In what ways can you relate to Peter's fear?*

He was afraid of the wind.
Jesus reached out & caught him.
afraid of what people will think.

5. *When Jesus calls you to do something, do you tend to react fearfully or boldly? Mark your answer on the continuum below. What kinds of spiritual activities help you to walk in greater boldness?*

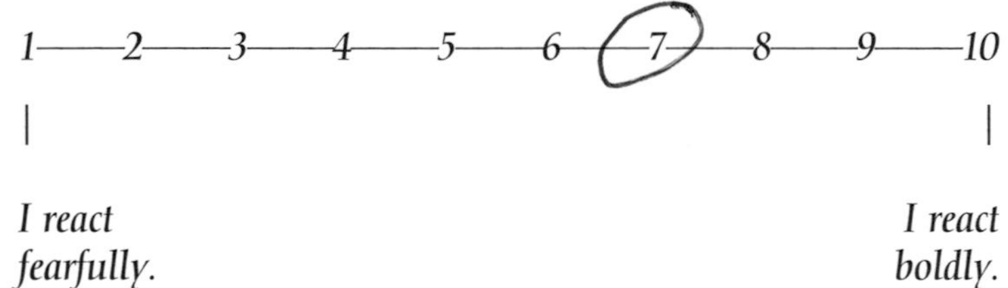

prayer & scripture & encouragement of other believers.

It may seem strange, but God actually calls us to develop a healthy fear of Him. This fear will not cause us to pull back from God but rather will move us forward in a more intimate and delightful relationship with Him.

6. *Look up the verses below. What does each passage reveal about the fear of the Lord?*

Isaiah 11:2–3: Delight in the fear of the Lord

Proverbs 1:7: The fear of the Lord is the beginning of wisdom

Proverbs 9:10: " "

Proverbs 15:33: wisdom's instruction is to fear the Lord.

Psalm 130:3–4: with reverence, we can serve Him.

The fear of the Lord should not be marked by despair—like the kind of fear we experience as a result of great heights or creepy spiders. Instead, we should fear the Lord out of an awestruck respect and honor for God. Trusting and loving our creator means we can't help but revere Him.

7. *Reflecting on the passages from the previous question, write out your own definition of a healthy fear of the Lord in the space below.*

8. *How can you more fully step out of a life full of fear that paralyzes toward a life full of a healthy fear of the Lord?*

While we aren't meant to live in fear, a healthy dose of fear helps keep us safe, allows us to walk in wisdom, and provides an appropriate understanding of our limitations.

Digging Deeper

Being fearful is not uncommon. In his letter to Timothy, Paul addressed this spirit of fear. Read **2 Timothy 1:7**. What spirit are we not meant to have? What spirit are we given? How does it make you feel to know that God has given you a spirit of power and love and sound mind? How can you embrace that God-given spirit? Spend some time in prayer asking God to fill you with His spirit and give you the grace and strength to overcome every fear that holds you back.

Bonus Activity

Find a friend who would be willing to help you confront one of your fears during the upcoming week. For example, if you're afraid of snakes, consider visiting the reptile exhibit at the zoo sometime this week. If you're afraid of being alone, try and spend a few hours this week in solitude. If you're afraid of being near water, ask a friend to sign up for a swimming lesson with you. Gently confront a fear in a safe, fun, and lighthearted way.

Five

A Healthy and Holy Dose of Anger

A man is as big as the things that make him angry.

WINSTON CHURCHILL,
BRITISH PRIME MINISTER

As she walked the slums of Nansana, Uganda, Shana Gilbert couldn't hold back her indignation at the injustice of what she saw. Hundreds of children slept on dirt floors, many of whom were abused and neglected. They had little to no clothing, no health care, and no way out. As the righteous anger brewed inside of her, Shana couldn't help but wonder, "What can I do?"

When Shana returned to her home in Colorado, the images of the children followed her. Though she was physically in America, her heart remained in Africa. Deep down inside, Shana knew she had to do something. She returned to Uganda and decided to launch a non-profit, grassroots organization focused on community development. Shana recognized the poverty was systemic for the children she grew to know and love. To save the children, she needed to address the way Ugandans live and think about their future. She began working alongside local Ugandans to create an intentional and sustainable foundation for economic and social change.

While working in Uganda, Shana became involved in caring for orphans. One little girl named Jesca captured Shana's heart. Before she was taken in by a ministry and cared for, the young girl had been begging for food on the side of the road and living under a tree. When Shana met Jesca she knew there was something special about her and later adopted her.

Anger can be a gift from God designed to awaken in us a desire for justice and caring for others.

Today, Shana's organization, Come Let's Dance, continues to work alongside Ugandans in a community outside of Kampala, Uganda. At their Slumbase—an acre of land outside the Katanga slums, they have created a self-sustaining farm, a medical clinic, and a new school.

Shana also sees the need for developing countries to empower and train women to have jobs and learn to provide for their families. Come Let's Dance created a program for women called Thread of Life. Thread of Life trains women to make and sell beautiful paper-bead jewelry, in order to establish a self-sustaining profession for these women. They desire to get to the root of the issues in order to end the cycle of poverty.

Shana's dream of developing a non-profit, community-development organization is coming to life. In 2011, she released her documentary, *Mzungu*, which was filmed on her first trip to Uganda—allowing her passion for Uganda to be seen worldwide. The community in Kampala, Uganda, is becoming sustainable from the ground up with the help of Shana and her team. Come Let's Dance is building up and training Ugandan leaders to take ownership in their country and their lifestyle—so fewer children will be homeless, unclothed, and unfed in the slums.

While we may be tempted to dismiss anger as an emotion we'd rather not feel, anger can be a gift from God designed to awaken in us a desire for justice and caring for others. Just as Shana was filled with anger at the injustice she witnessed, we, too, can use anger at injustice as a source of courage to defend the defenseless and give voice to those who cannot speak for themselves.

1. *When have you had an encounter that stirred anger toward injustice? How did you respond?*

2. *Make a list of five things you've been angry about over the course of the past month. Did the anger you experienced compel you toward a righteous action or an unrighteous behavior?*

In John 2, Jesus displayed a righteous anger in response to injustice. As the Jews travelled to Jerusalem for the Passover pilgrimage, Jesus was appalled by the injustice He saw. As Jesus entered the temple—a place of purity—anger bubbled inside of Him toward what He witnessed.

3. *Read* **John 2:13–17**. *What injustice caused Jesus to become angry? What was Jesus' response to the injustice He saw in the temple?*

Just as Jesus was angered at the injustice and disobedience He witnessed in the temple, we, too, are often angered by the injustices we see. However, Jesus did not sin in His anger. Instead, He did something to right the situation.

4. *Is a response like Jesus' to the moneychangers ever appropriate in our modern world? Why or why not? Explain. What would be a modern equivalent of Jesus' response to the moneychangers?*

While God gifts us with the ability to feel anger, sometimes we become angry at the wrong things. The Bible gives us many wise instructions against unhealthy anger.

5. *Look up the following verses and record the wisdom each passage offers regarding how to handle anger. Which of these pieces of wisdom on how to handle anger has been most helpful to you? Why?*

   James 1:19–20:

   Ephesians 4:26:

   Proverbs 14:29:

   Matthew 5:22–24:

We are instructed to control our anger because, if left unchecked, anger can get the best of us. One passage about two brothers ends in murder because one brother could not control his unhealthy anger toward the other.

6. *Take turns reading* **Genesis 4:1–16**. *What caused Cain's anger (hint: vv. 4–5)? What situations in the past week have caused you to respond in anger?*

While Bible scholars debate why Cain's offering was unacceptable, many believe it was because Cain's sacrifice was not from the absolute best of his crops. Others believe it was because his offering wasn't a blood sacrifice. Either way, the significance of this passage is found in Cain's reaction.

7. *What were the consequences for Cain's action (hint: vv. 11–16)? When in the past two weeks have you become angry and allowed the anger to get the best of you? What resulted?*

When unbridled, anger can get the best of us, but when bridled, anger can give us the courage to stand up for injustice and give voice to the voiceless.

8. *Are there any areas in your life where you sense God compelling you to pursue justice on behalf of someone else? What changes in your life do you need to make to have a more healthy response toward anger?*

While we may be tempted to dismiss anger as an emotion we'd rather not feel, anger can be a gift from God designed to awaken in us a desire for justice and caring for others.

Digging Deeper

Read **Mark 10:13–16**. Within this passage, what provoked Jesus' anger? How was Jesus' response to the disciples and the children an expression of love? Spend some time prayerfully reflecting on how you can exhibit Christ's love when difficult situations arise.

Bonus Activity

Do you have an organization or ministry you're passionate about in regard to pursuing justice for others? Research your favorite organization and share about it for a few minutes with the group next week. To learn more about Shana and Come Let's Dance or to purchase jewelry from Thread of Life, visit www.comeletsdance.org.

Six

The Unexpected Gift of Sadness

Tomorrow, if all literature was to be destroyed and it was left to me to retain one work only, I should save Job.

VICTOR HUGO,
AUTHOR

The book of Job is part of the wisdom literature of the Old Testament, along with Proverbs, Ecclesiastes, and Song of Solomon. It tells the story of a wealthy, successful man living in the land of Uz who had seven sons and three daughters. The story opens with an insight into Job's character. When Job learned that his children may have inadvertently sinned, he offered sacrifices on their behalf—an example that Job was a righteous man who loved God.

In an unusual twist, an adversary (often thought of as Satan) approached God about Job. Satan claimed that the only reason Job was righteous and loved God was because Job had been successful and prosperous. If stripped of his possessions, Satan argued, Job wouldn't be as faithful to God. Out of this heavenly court scene would come an unforgettable test for Job whom, according to God's command,

Satan would be allowed to strip Job of all his material blessings. At Satan's request, Job would be allowed to lose everything—everything, said the Lord, except for his life.

Almost immediately, Job lost all of his children when a mighty wind caused the house of his oldest child to collapse while all of Job's children were gathered there for a feast. Every single one of Job's children died. Soon after, Job lost his sheep and servants to a fire that fell from heaven. Bandits stole Job's remaining livestock. However, instead of responding in bitterness and anger, Job declared, "Naked I came from my mother's womb, and naked shall I return there. The LORD gave, and the LORD has taken away; blessed be the name of the LORD" (Job 1:21).

In response to Satan's request, God allowed Job to lose everything except his life.

Despite his tremendous loss and pain, Job's trials had only begun. The calamities continued. Job's body broke out in painful boils. Sitting in ashes, Job resorted to scraping his skin with broken pottery to alleviate the pain.

When Job turned to his friends for comfort, he found their responses disheartening and discouraging. His friends Eliphaz, Bildad, and Zophar reasoned that Job's losses must have been a result of sin—a kind of retribution theology or punishment. Though the trio couldn't identify which sin Job had committed, they were convinced that God rewarded good and punished evil without exception. Job maintained that he was innocent. He had not sinned, but rather than accuse God of wrong, Job continued to seek God for an explanation. The conversation circled round and round the issues of sin, justice, God's sovereignty, and mercy until God finally spoke in the form of a cloud or whirlwind.

God's response took the form of rhetorical questions that challenged Job to recognize God's power in creating and holding the world together. God made it clear that He did not need creation's approval because He was the creator and maintained freedom and sovereignty over all. God defended Job from his friends who were unhelpful and misguided, and upheld Job as a righteous servant.

At the end of his story, Job, who held on to faith through all the tragedy and heartache he faced, was blessed with seven more sons and three more beautiful daughters. All of Job's wealth and possessions doubled what he had lost, and he lived another 140 years, having the privilege of seeing his children to the fourth generation. Job died wealthy and satisfied with life at an old age.

Job experienced loss and pain marked by sadness and mourning, but even in the midst of the discouragement and depression, he chose to honor God. In all of our lives, the question is not if we will experience loss and pain and feel sadness, but how will we respond when we do? Job's example encourages us that even when we don't understand, God is still in control. Even though we may be tempted to question or doubt, God is still good. And though we experience hardship and challenges, God uses those times to draw us into a more intimate relationship with Himself and reveal Him to us in unexpected ways.

1. *Read* ***Job 1****. How did God's and Satan's views of Job differ? Under the terms of the agreement reached between God and Satan, who was really in control of the situation?*

God saw Job as blameless & upright, a man who feared God & shunned evil. Satan saw him as a man protected from everything & blessed with so much. God only allowed it & would not allow Job to be killed.

2. *What was taken away from Job that made him experience loss, pain, and great sadness (hint: vv. 13–19)? What could be taken away from you that would lead you to experience the greatest pain, loss, and sadness?*

His livestock, servants, children

When Satan approached God a second time, God noted that Job remained righteous and full of integrity even after his family and prosperity were stripped away. Satan argued that if Job's health was removed, then Job would curse God. After listening to Satan's argument, God allowed Satan to afflict Job with physical suffering, but again Job's life would be spared. Job's body was afflicted with sores all over his body. The physical pain must have been tremendous, because Job sat in ashes scraping his wounds with shards of pottery. The remaining friends and family of Job offered their responses.

3. *Read* **Job 2**. *In the space below, record how Job's wife and friends responded to Job's great loss and sadness:*

Job's wife (vv. 9–10):

Curse God & die!

Job's friends (vv. 11–13):

They wept & sat with him & said nothing.

4. *When you've experienced a time of great loss, pain, or sadness, what are some of the most helpful things people have said and done for you? What are some of the most harmful things people have said and done for you?*

5. *According to the following passages, what was Job's attitude and response toward the suffering he had to endure? How would your response to Job's situation been different?*

Job 1:20–22:

Job 9:1–24:

Job 13:15:

Job 42:2:

Job's friends, Eliphaz, Bildad, and Zophar, in their attempts to offer help to Job, began trying to determine reasons for Job's suffering. Their response to Job's situation turned to cold analysis and harsh accusations. The real insight into Job's situation emerged only when God appeared and began asking questions rather than offering answers.

6. *Look up the following passages in the chart below. What questions did God ask Job in each one? What does each question reveal about God?*

Scripture	What God Asked Job	What Is Revealed about God
Job 38:4	Where were you when I created the earth?	God created the earth
Job 38:8	Who shut up the sea behind doors	God controls the seas.
Job 38:12	Have you ever given orders to the morning...	He makes the sun rise
Job 38:18	Have you comprehended the vast	God understands everything about the earth.
Job 38:19	What is the way to the abode. . .	God controls dark & light
Job 38:22	Have you entered. . . .	God created snow & hail.
Job 38:24–25	what is the way to the. . .	God controls the weather
Job 38:29	From whose womb. . . .	God controls ice & frost
Job 38:32	Can you bring forth. . .	God commands the stars & animals
Job 38:36–37	Who gives the ibis wisdom. . .	God created wisdom.
Job 38:41	who provides food for. . . .	God cares & provides for his creation.

In His sovereignty and power, God allowed Job to experience pain, loss, and sadness.

7. *Read* **Job 42:1–6**. *What important insights did Job learn about God through this difficult journey? What important insights have you learned about God through difficult journeys in your life?*

He thought he knew who God was, but his perspective changed.

8. *Read* **Job 36:16** *alongside of* **Job 42:5–6**. *When have you experienced a season of loss, pain, and sadness that drew you into a more intimate relationship with God?*

my time as an adolescent when mom was sick & I had so much responsibility at such a young age

On a list of emotions we try to avoid, sadness often tops the list. Yet not only is feeling sad normal, it's a gift from God. Sadness prompts us to pray, reminds us that we need others, calls us to be honest with ourselves and God, and creates compassion for others in our hearts.

Digging Deeper

Read Job 42. What role did Job's remaining friends and family play in Job's healing? Who has been the greatest source of comfort to you during difficult times? Who have you reached out to during difficult times as a source of comfort? What prevents you from being available for others? they comforted & consoled him.

CHALLENGE!

Bonus Activity

God invites us to be a comfort to those who are facing difficult circumstances and challenging situations. Over the course of the next week, spend some time reflecting on Galatians 6:2 and 2 Corinthians 1:3–4. Then prayerfully consider a practical way you can be a source of comfort to someone you know who is facing difficult times. Share your experience with the group during your next gathering.

Before Bonus Activity:
Read highlighted portion,
Then Read Job 19:25-27

Emotions That Make Life Fuller

God gives us emotions that fill our life with surprise, joy, and celebration. Without such delightful emotions, we couldn't experience the fullness of all God has for us.

Seven

A Holy Surprise

Life is not measured by the number of breaths we take, but by the moments that take our breath away.

Unknown

Did you know that surprise is an emotion? And it's one that fills life with excitement and anticipation. Surprises come in all forms and fashions, but they always catch us off guard—in a good way. One of the greatest surprises for all of humanity was the arrival of Jesus. Though the Jews knew the Messiah was coming, they had no idea when or how He would arrive. Jesus' entrance into the world demonstrated the unexpected ways in which God leads, guides, and moves in our world.

Sometimes God takes us by total surprise and teaches us through the most unexpected circumstances. Take the following Holiday Surprise Quiz to gain insight into your threshold for surprise throughout the year.

Special Occasion Surprise Quiz

1. *For Valentine's Day, your beloved has planned a romantic date but refuses to tell you where you're going or what you will be doing. As you prepare for the evening, what is going through your mind?*

   a. You're wondering what he has planned.

   b. You're listening to romantic songs as you add a touch of lip gloss.

   c. You're trying on outfits, frustrated he didn't give you a hint on how to dress.

2. *You just got off the phone with your aunt. It's July 2, and they have just called to share some great news. They have won an all-expense-paid cruise to the Caribbean for the entire extended family this Fourth of July weekend. You have a day and a half to get the whole family packed and ready for a three-day cruise. What are you most likely to do first?*

   a. Start emptying every hamper and begin washing clothes like a mad woman.

   b. Look up the ship online and plan activities for each port of call.

   c. Tell your family that they'll just have to enjoy a great time without you!

3. *Your soon-to-be-fourteen-year-old niece has been babysitting for your kids throughout the summer and you know her birthday is coming up soon. How do you approach the planning?*

   a. Enlist her best friend to help with the details and invites.

   b. Start spinning a web of varying possibilities now, so she won't know what the party theme will be.

c. Put it off a little while longer, hoping a theme or party plan will come to you in the shower or in the middle of the night or sometime other than now.

4. *You agree to host Thanksgiving dinner at your home this year. You carefully plan the menu and start making practice pies a few weeks out. You make cute little name cards for each seat, and everything is absolutely perfect when it's time for the guests to arrive. When your brother knocks on the door, you see that he has not come alone as you assumed he would, but has brought his girlfriend and her brother as well. How are you likely to react?*

   a. You smile and act as gracious as you can as you add a card table to the already crowded dining room.

   b. You send the kids to their playroom and tell them to quickly make two extra name cards while you scoot the chairs closer together and set the extra plates at the table.

   c. You pull your brother aside and ask him why on earth he didn't mention that he was bringing two extra mouths to feed.

5. *Your best girlfriend invites you out to dinner. You think you're just going to have a catch-up session at a restaurant. But as you're checking Facebook before you head out, you accidentally see that she's planning to surprise you with tickets for a sold-out show by the reunited boy band you both used to love. What is most likely to go through your mind when you make the discovery?*

   a. You decide to casually pretend nothing has changed and throw some earplugs into your purse just in case.

   b. You are upset that you found out ahead of time and hope you can fake the surprised face of delight you have now when she finally tells you the real plan.

c. You are upset that she lied to you and wish you weren't going to have to stay out so late on a work night.

6. *It's a week before Christmas, and all through the house not a creature is stirring . . . except for you! You're up tippy-toeing through the wrapping paper and trying not to wake the rest of the family. What are you most likely doing?*

a. Regretting that last cup of coffee and heading to the restroom again.

b. Making sure all the rest of the house is asleep and not peaking at the amazing gifts you bought them.

c. Rewrapping the package you just opened exactly the way it was so no one will know you've been spying on your own gifts.

Scoring

Give yourself 1 point for every A, 2 points for every B, and 0 points for every C answer. Add the total together and read below for your results.

If you scored between 0 and 3, you are a surprise minimalist. You make careful plans for your life and those you love. You didn't get to where you are in life by leaving things up to chance, and you spend energy trying to minimize the risk of unexpected surprises. People love to be around you because you are steady and dependable. While your discipline is enviable and very impressive, be sure to be flexible when surprises do come your way.

If you scored between 4 and 7, you are a surprise moderate. You can roll with the flow or fly by the seat of your pants. Either way, you are flexible and easygoing. People feel at ease around you, and nothing seems to rattle your cage. You'll happily take surprises that come your way, but you won't go out of your way to seek them out. While your easygoing nature is admirable and encouraging to others, be sure to practice the art of surprising others with words or actions of kindness.

If you scored between 8 and 12, you are a surprise maven. Not only do you love being surprised, you enjoy surprising others as well. You are full of life and exciting to be around. People appreciate your zest for life and carefree attitude. And you can change plans quickly when the unexpected arises. That is a special gift. While you can seemingly adjust to new situations in a flash, be sure to remember that everyone is not as quickly adaptable. Have patience with those who do not like constant surprise, and be ready when an unexpected friendship with someone not like you arises.

1. *How did you score on the Holiday Surprise Quiz? Did anything surprise you or catch your attention about your personal results? If so, explain.*

2. *What are some of the challenges that emerge whenever you're caught by surprise in the following areas?*

   In your home . . .

   In your family . . .

   In your workplace . . .

   In your everyday life . . .

3. *Read* **Luke 1**. *In the following chart, write out who was surprised in each passage and what surprised them:*

Scripture	Who Was Surprised	The Surprise
Luke 1:9		
Luke 1:11–12		
Luke 1:13–15		
Luke 1:20		
Luke 1:21–22		
Luke 1:24–25		
Luke 1:28–29		
Luke 1:31		
Luke 1:34–35		
Luke 1:41		
Luke 1:63		
Luke 1:64–66		

The births of Jesus and John the Baptist were filled with surprises for everyone who watched the events unfold. The surprises or unexpected turns alerted everyone to God's presence and faithfulness.

4. *Why do you think God surprises His people so often throughout the Scriptures?*

5. *Read* **Matthew 7:11** *and* **James 1:17–18**. *In the last three months, when has God surprised you with a good gift? How did you respond?*

6. *Do you find yourself more surprised by the extraordinary and miraculous activities of God in your life or by the more ordinary and everyday? Explain.*

7. *Read* **Isaiah 63:7**. *Why is it important to celebrate the good surprises and unexpected kindness that God shows you? What prevents you from sharing the goodness and kindness God has shown you with others?*

8. *How can you be more intentional about celebrating the surprises and unexpected things God wants to do in your life?*

Surprise may be one of the most delightful and unexpected gifts God gives us. God often surprises us and leaves us in awe of His mercy, compassion, kindness, and goodness.

Digging Deeper

In the book of Acts, Luke recorded a moment when everyone was surprised by God. Read Acts 12:6–19. Who do you think was most surprised by the events of this story? When have you been surprised by an answer to prayer? Do you pray with the expectation to be surprised by God with the answer? Why or why not?

Bonus Activity

Surprise someone this week. Bake fresh cookies or bread for someone who is sick or can't get out of the house. Take a neighbor to lunch. Kidnap a friend for a quick manicure. Surprise someone with an act of kindness.

Eight

Contagious Joy

I've learned that people will forget what you said, people will forget what you did, but people will never forget how you made them feel.

Maya Angelou,
former poet laureate

Have you ever been around someone who just exuded joy? You know the type . . . her glass always seems to be half full? Her smile seems to be a message from deep within rather than a simple facial expression. She has a love for life and a love for people that remains steady through all her own good and bad times.

Joy is a tiny little word that is often misunderstood in a big way. It is easy to confuse the word *joy* with *happiness*, and they do have similarities. They're like best friends. Where you find one, you often find the other, and these are absolutely the kind of BFFs we need in our lives! The writer of Ecclesiastes emphasized the importance of living a happy life in Ecclesiastes 3:12: "Nothing is better for them than to rejoice, and to do good in their lives."

True joy runs so much deeper into the soul than any amount of happiness could. Happiness, after all, is fleeting. You can easily be happy one minute and not happy the next. But the joy that comes from the Lord lasts forever and is consistently present regardless of circumstance or situation.

This kind of joy has a superbly positive effect on everyone around. It's contagious. You just feel better about life after being exposed to joy, even in small doses. A research study performed by Harvard and MIT researchers documented that the spread of happiness (or sadness) is absolutely contagious, with spreading patterns very similar to communicable diseases like the flu.

The spread of happiness is absolutely contagious, with spreading patterns very similar to communicable diseases like the flu.

But here's the best part—being full of joy is not only good for those around you, it's actually good for your own body and soul as well. Researchers have conducted multiple studies associated with joy that scientifically prove there is physical benefit in being joyful. An article from BBC, for example, cites a group of American psychologists who discovered that positive thinkers live 7.5 years longer than their more pessimistic counterparts.[1] Having a positive attitude toward aging proved to have even greater effect than physiological measures like blood pressure and cholesterol. And a University of Maryland School of Medicine study concluded that laughter helps blood vessels stay healthier.[2]

So for a healthy body *and* a healthy soul, take the advice of one of the Bible's wisest prophets, Nehemiah, and let the joy of the Lord be your strength (Nehemiah 8:10). Joy is a gift and one that God loves to give us, especially as we put our complete trust in Him. Let's be honest. All of us have room in our lives for a little bit more joy. We

can experience more joy as we spend more time in God's presence and allow the Holy Spirit to produce fruit in us as we walk in obedience to Him.

1. *Make a list of three people you know whom you'd describe as "full of joy." What are some of the common characteristics they share in their approach to life, their attitude, and their expressions of faith?*

   Julie, Gayle, Kendra, Melissa
   looking for the positive side
   Know they can't control their
   situation, but Know God can.

2. *When have you been influenced by someone who was bubbling over with joy? How did their attitude and outlook specifically affect you?*

   It helps my attitude,
   unless they're being fake.

3. *When have you been influenced by someone who lacked joy of any kind? How did their negative attitude and outlook affect you?*

   It's easy to pick up their
   negativity toward life
   & circumstances.

4. *Look up the following passages. What does each one reveal about joy?*

Scripture	Insight on Joy
Psalm 16:11	You will fill me w/ joy in your presence
Psalm 5:11	Sing for joy
Psalm 33:1	Sing joyfully to the Lord
Psalm 90:14	sing for joy & be glad all our days
1 Chronicles 16:27	joy is in his dwelling place
Zephaniah 3:17	He will rejoice over you w/singing
Galatians 5:22–23	Joy is a fruit of the Spirit.

5. *What role does the joy of the Lord play in your own life right now? If your attitude is contagious, what are people around you catching?*

I can sing for joy for God is Good (all the time).
I hope they like being around me & want what I have.

Paul and Barnabus faced continuous persecution as they traveled around spreading the Word of God. When they were driven out of Antioch by those who opposed their message, Paul and Barnabus must have been sad and even a bit discouraged as they shook the dust from their feet and left town. But even in their difficult

situation, they had joy deep within because of their trust in God. Though they encountered great persecution and pain, the Scripture says they were "filled with joy." They knew that God's presence was with them and His will would be accomplished in spite of any temporary trial.

6. *Read* Acts 13:47–52. *In the midst of trials, Paul and Barnabus were filled with joy and the Holy Spirit. When have you gone through a difficult situation in the past year but found yourself filled with joy?*

When our best friends felt the need to leave the church, but God gave me peace about the situation.

Despite the challenges Paul and Barnabas faced, they continued to persevere with great joy. As a result, a great number of Jews and Gentiles believed.

7. *Read* Acts 14:1–7. *What could have happened if the discouragement from the previous town had prevented Paul and Barnabas from continuing their work? What kinds of situations or circumstances tempt you to give up?*

They would never have reached all those people for the Lord. It's tempting to give up on the church!

8. *In what areas of your life do you need to experience more of the joy of the Lord right now?*

In the conflict & life of our church.

> *The Lord desires to be the source of the joy and hope that strengthens us regardless of our circumstances.*

Digging Deeper

Read **John 15:9–11**. What correlation do you see in Jesus' words between love for the Father and joy? What does it look like for you personally to have joy that is "full"? What does remaining in God's love look like for you on a daily basis?

Bonus Activity

Since joy is contagious, take some time this week to purposefully spread joy to others. Encourage a coworker. Speak positively to a person in the service industry. Write a note to a friend. Smile at a stranger. Be mindful of the attitude you are sharing with others.

Nine

The Wonders of the Calm

We ourselves know by experience that there is no place for comfort like the cross. It is a tree stripped of all foliage, and apparently dead; yet we sit under its shadow with great delight, and its fruit is sweet unto our taste.

C. H. Spurgeon

Like many dogs, Jake fears nothing more than thunderstorms. This eighty-pound chocolate lab may seem strong and fearless, but as soon as thunder claps, whimpers and whines fill the house. Whenever storm clouds start brewing—growing darker and more ominous, Jake can be found, tail between his legs, darting inside to find a safe spot to hide. Usually, he tucks himself between his owner's legs or directly against their knees.

One particularly stormy spring day, Sarah—Jake's owner—leaves work. She hustles to her car holding a magazine over her head, annoyed that she'd left her umbrella in the car. As she counts the seconds between the lightning flash and the clap of thunder, she worries about Jake who is probably terrified by this storm. She tries to hurry home to make sure he's okay.

As she walks inside, she checks all of Jake's usual hiding spots. Behind the couch—no Jake. Atop the bed—no Jake. The loving companion doesn't respond to her calling either. As she heads into the kitchen to call the neighbors, she nearly trips over her blender—sprawled across the kitchen floor. Surrounding the blender are pots and pans, baking sheets, and a toaster. All of the items from the lower kitchen cabinet have been emptied. When she opens the cabinet door, Jake's beady brown eyes glow in the darkness—Jake has found a safe place to hide from the storm. Sarah calls Jake out from his hiding spot and holds him until the storm subsides.[1]

God is the source of comfort no matter what storm of life we may be facing.

Just like Jake, sometimes it is easy to let our fears control and consume us. However, throughout Scripture we are encouraged to fear not. We are reminded that God not only created everything but has power over all things. God is sovereign and an ever-present help in time of need. God is the source of comfort no matter what storm of life we may be facing.

Jake found comfort in his master's protection—just as we find comfort in God's embrace. The Scripture is chock-full of passages expressing God as the source of comfort in our times of need. Understanding our desire for calm—our need for refuge away from the chaos of life—allows us to seek comfort in the shelter of the almighty God. As we learn to delight in peace and rest, we can discern new facets of God's character that we could never fathom otherwise.

1. *Have you ever had a pet, like Jake, who behaved in unusual or zany ways? If so, describe.*

2. *Have you ever had a pet that reminded you or taught you a principle that was true about God? If so, describe.*

God desires to be our shield and our comfort in our times of need. As He placed the stars in the sky and breathed life onto the earth, His desire was not for chaos and pain. Instead, God rules over the chaos of life and invites us to embrace calmness and peace.

3. *Take turns reading* **Genesis 1**. *What comfort do you find in knowing that God created all things? That God has power over all things? When are you tempted to believe that something is beyond God's power or reach?*

The God of the universe, who created all things, also has power over all things. Nothing is beyond His comprehension or grasp. Even in the literary structure of Genesis 1, we see God's power and order of all creation.

4. *Fill in the chart below using Genesis 1. What strikes you as interesting about this chart? (Hint: **Notice the way the chart is divided up and the similarities between days 1 and 4, 2 and 5, and 3 and 6.**)*

What Was Formed		What It Was Filled With	
Day 1:	day + nite	Day 4:	sun, moon stars
Day 2:	sky + water	Day 5:	fish + birds
Day 3:	land-vegetation	Day 6:	all living creatures

God created the earth and everything in it with a perfect purpose and order. What may seem like chaos to us is completely under control by the Creator. When Jesus walked the earth, He understood the pain and discomfort we often experience. In one conversation to a crowd in Israel, He offered a warm and comforting invitation to His followers.

5. *Read **Matthew 11:28–30**. What comfort does Jesus offer in this passage? How do these words of comfort directly ease you in light of the events of the past week?*

Jesus' provision of a light and easy burden reveals the Father's plan for the redemption of humanity—not a world of chaos and weariness, but one of rest and intimacy with our Creator. Even when we are in our greatest discomfort, we have the Holy Spirit speaking on our behalf.

6. *Read* **Romans 8:26–27***. When in the last month have you experienced not knowing what to pray for? When have you experienced the Holy Spirit intervening and speaking for you on your behalf?*

7. *How do you feel knowing that God the Father, Jesus, and the Holy Spirit long to be the source of your comfort?*

8. *What steps can you take during the upcoming week to embrace the calmness God wants to give you?*

We can find comfort in God. No matter what storms of life we're experiencing, God wants to give us a sense of His calmness.

Digging Deeper

Read **Psalm 91**. Take out a journal. Write down all the words of this psalm that offer comfort. What image of God is the psalmist drawing in your head throughout the words of this psalm? What does it mean in your own life to seek refuge and shelter in God? Spend time in prayer asking God to reveal Himself to you as the God of comfort and calm.

Bonus Activity

Be a comforter! Once we are filled with the comfort offered by God, we then can become comforters. This week, find a friend, neighbor, or family member who is in need of comfort and calm and find a way to help them. Offer free babysitting, make a meal for them, lend a listening ear, or just write them a note of encouragement. Share your experience comforting with the group next week.

Adorning Emotions with Love

Whatever emotions we may be feeling, they need to be dressed in love. When we love, we wrap our emotions in the care and protection they need not only to heal but also to be a source of healing to others.

Ps 56:3
When I

Ten

Growing in Trust

God is God. Because He is God, He is worthy of my trust and obedience. I will find rest nowhere but in His holy will, a will that is unspeakably beyond my largest notions of what He is up to.

Elisabeth Elliot,
Christian author

Glancing outside her window, she noticed the sun high in the sky—midday. Perfect. No one else would be at the well. She loaded up her jar and walked through the scorching heat toward Jacob's well. She avoided the passing glances of judgment from the windows of her neighbors—people who either mocked or disregarded her. They wanted nothing to do with her, so she avoided them at all costs, which is why she drew water in the heat of the day, when no one else would be at the well. Or so she thought.

As she approached the well, she noticed a man leaning against the edge of the well. She didn't recognize Him and figured He must be new to town. She decided to ignore His presence and began to draw water. But the man refused to ignore her and proceeded to ask her a question: "Will you give Me a drink?"

She was taken aback by the bold request. After all, Jews and Samaritans never got along. "You are a Jew and I'm a Samaritan woman. How can You ask me for a drink?" she inquired.

Though the woman didn't know what to think or even if she should trust the man, he continued to reassure her and revealed himself as the long-awaited Messiah.

The man didn't hesitate in His reply. "If you knew the gift of God and who it is that asks you for a drink, you would have asked Him and He would have given you living water."

The man went on to describe mysterious water that promised to quench thirst once and for all. What? Living water? The woman had travelled to the well countless times to fill her water satchel. Now a stranger was offering a supernatural kind of water that meant she'd never have to return to the well.

But before the man would give her any of the promised water, He made an unexpected request: "Go, call your husband and come back."

The woman felt a huge lump in her throat. She admitted that she didn't have a husband. Then the man told her something He couldn't have known on His own: she had five husbands and the man she was currently with wasn't one of them.

Who was this man who knew so much? Who offered eternal life? Could the man really be the Messiah?

Though the woman didn't know what to think or even if she should trust the man, he continued to reassure her and revealed himself as the long-awaited Messiah.

After so many disappointments and heartaches in her relationships with men, the woman at the well struggled with trust. She wondered who and what to believe. Yet Jesus met her one unsuspecting day and restored her trust in God. Jesus revealed Himself as the Messiah. Once the woman encountered Jesus, she couldn't contain the good news. She headed back to her village to tell anyone and everyone who would listen. As a result, many Samaritans believed in Jesus.

Like the Samaritan woman, we've all had experiences and encounters in our pasts that make us hesitant to trust. But God invites us to trust Him with everything. God is our refuge and strength, the one who always remains trustworthy no matter what happens in life.

1. *Read* **John 4**. *What is one of the most significant situations or events in your life that has affected your willingness to trust others?*

2. *In the last three months, what situation or event has caused you to second-guess whether or not you can trust someone or something?*

3. *Judging from your own experiences, how can a lack of trust negatively affect your relationships?*

It's hard to have relationships if you are unable to trust.

We all have people in our lives who have broken our trust, but we all have access to place our trust in the God who desires to be our refuge and strength. The writer of Psalm 73 had his trust broken. He'd seen injustice, the wicked triumphing, and the evil surrounding him; and he had no reason to trust anyone, until he entered the sanctuary of God. Then he found healing and a change of perspective.

4. *Read* **Psalm 73***. What trust did the psalmist have broken? What brought healing for the psalmist?*

26 my flesh + my heart may fail, but God is the strength of my heart & my portion forever.

5. *What has been the biggest source of healing for the broken trust you've experienced in your life?*

6. *Fill in the chart below, noticing what each of the following passages reveals about trust and explaining how you've found these passages to be true in your own life.*

Scripture	Reveals About Trust	True in Your Life
Proverbs 30:5	Every word of God is flawless	reading His word
2 Samuel 22:31	God's way is perfect	
Psalm 36:7	God's love is unfailing	you can
Psalm 118:8	Better to trust God than humans	always trust God.

7. *Read* **Isaiah 31:1**. *What are some unhealthy things in your own life that you're tempted to place your trust in?*

8. *Read* **Proverbs 3:5–6**. *When are you most tempted to lean on your own understanding and pick your own path? What intentional steps do you need to take in your own life to grow in your trust of God?*

God invites us to place our trust in Him. When we trust in God, we will never be abandoned or disappointed.

Digging Deeper

One of the various genres of psalms are psalms of praise. Read **Psalm 146**. What does the author of this psalm warn against? When is a time you have found yourself putting your trust in humans? What was the result? Instead, who does the psalmist say to place trust in? When have you taken the psalmist's advice? What was the outcome?

Bonus Activity

One of the most challenging aspects of broken trust is forgiving the people who have broken your trust. Sometime over the course of the next week, spend time prayerfully making a list of people who have broken your trust. Include co-workers, family members, and friends from the past and present. Then spend time forgiving each person and praying a blessing over them.

Eleven

Hopeful and Hope-Filled

Start by doing what is necessary;
then do what's possible; and suddenly
you are doing the impossible.

St. Francis of Assisi

Times were hard for William Kamkwamba. His family was on the brink of starvation in Malawi. William was forced to drop out of school at the age of fourteen because his parents couldn't afford for him to continue. The school tuition of eighty dollars per year had to go toward basic survival needs instead. Drought and poverty had stolen all sense of hope from this hardworking family.

William returned home from school and tried to help his family in the maize (corn) fields, but the severe lack of water yielded a dismal harvest. But William found himself hungry for more than food. He was hungry for knowledge. Hungry for hope. Hungry for the possibility of a better tomorrow. He spent every free moment tucked into a small public library in his village trying to continue his studies on his own.

One day William stumbled upon a tattered old textbook in the library that contained a photograph of a windmill. He was instantly captivated. William had never seen anything like it, but the book claimed the odd-looking contraption could actually generate electricity. Since only 2 percent of Malawians had access to electricity, William had grown up without it but knew the difference electricity could make in his home and in his village.

When it came to the dire situation his community faced, William looked to what was possible instead of what was impossible.

Studying the photograph and text carefully, something sparked inside of him. William decided to build a windmill himself. Slowly, he gathered trash and discarded metal pieces. He scoured the village for old bicycle parts, stereos, and rubber from worn-out flip-flops. Like a modern-day Noah, William worked tirelessly on an object none of the neighbors had ever seen before. Many of the onlookers believed William must have been on drugs or gone loony from the lack of nourishment.

William was a young man on a mission. And one day he crawled up to the top of his rickety tower and harnessed enough wind power to light up a light bulb. Before long, William figured out how to light up his family's home with light bulbs. Then he figured out a way to provide electricity for the entire village. With his skills and knowledge flourishing, he went on to install a solar-powered mechanical pump. Today, life-saving water is available for the local people and their crops. A new hope sprung up in this small African village.[1]

When it came to the dire situation his community faced, William could have seen the glass half empty, but he chose to see it as half full. He looked to what was possible instead of what was impossible.

As believers, we are to look to God in impossible situations and by faith begin to see the glass half full. What seems impossible from our human perspective is possible for almighty God. Just as the knowledge of a potential harnessing of the wind gave hope to William, simply knowing God is God can and should give us an unshakeable hope as well.

Hope is an essential emotion—one we all need. Maybe that's one reason the Bible reminds us repeatedly of the importance of hope. Throughout the Scripture, we're reminded that God is our steady, powerful source of hope. And hope can make a world of difference in our hearts and the lives of those around us.

1. *When have you seen someone in your community or family overcome impossible odds?*

when Sandra was pregnant w/twins.

Throughout Scripture, we see examples of men and women, like William, who have great hope for their futures. One profound example of someone who hoped in the Lord is found in the gospel of Mark.

2. *Read* Mark 5:24–34. *What does this passage reveal about the woman's health and condition (hint: vv. 26–27)?*

She had spent years + all her money to get better + she was getting worse.

3. *Read* **Leviticus 15:25–31**. *Reflecting on this passage, what hardships do you think the woman in the story from Mark 5 faced emotionally, relationally, and socially?*

She was thought to be unclean & impure.

4. *How was this woman blessed and rewarded for placing her hope in Jesus? When have you experienced a similar blessing?*

She was healed.

5. *The miracle of the woman's healing occurred in the middle of another story. Read* **Mark 5:21–23, 35–43**. *What similarities and differences do you find between the two stories? What do these stories reveal about the importance of placing our hope in Christ?*

all earthly things had ~~faith~~ failed, but Jesus healed & raised from the dead.

6. *Match the scriptures below with the blessings and rewards of hope found in each. In the third column, describe how you have experienced similar blessings and rewards after placing your hope in the Lord.*

Scripture	Blessings and Rewards of Hope	Your Experience
Psalm 31:24	Let your heart take courage.	
Psalm 33:18	The eye of the Lord is on those who fear Him.	
Psalm 146:5	Blessed is He whose help is the God of Jacob.	
Proverbs 10:28	The hope of the righteous brings joy	
1 Thessalonians 4:13	others grieve because they have no hope	

7. *Hoping in the Lord isn't always easy. When do you find it most difficult to place your hope in God?*

While hoping in the Lord may be a scary idea, God desires us to place our hope in Him and Him alone.

8. *How can you focus on being intentional about placing your hope in the Lord this week? What does hoping in the Lord look like for you at this stage of your life?*

Hope is an essential emotion—one we can't live without. When we combine hope with faith, we find ourselves joyfully trusting God with everything.

Digging Deeper

Read Romans 15:13. In his letter to the church in Rome, Paul specifically prayed for the Romans to have the joy and peace that comes from hope. How have you experienced the "God of hope" as Paul described? According to Paul, what is the source of our hope? When have you experienced this to be true in your life? How can you focus on being intentional about placing your hope in the Lord this week?

Bonus Activity

Just like the hopeless woman described in Mark 5:24–34, there are people in our lives who desperately need the hope of Jesus. Select three friends or family members who may need to "touch Jesus' cloak." Spend time sharing Jesus with these people this week.

Twelve

Abounding in Love

It is easy to love the people far away. It is not always easy to love those close to us. It is easier to give a cup of rice to relieve hunger than to relieve the loneliness of pain of someone unloved in our own home. Bring love into your home for this is where our love for each other must start.

Mother Teresa,
Nobel Peace Prize winner

Jesus spent the majority of His time with a dozen followers whom He pulled aside on multiple occasions to share special lessons and teachable moments. Of the twelve, three were particularly close to Jesus: Peter, James, and John. Of those three, one disciple seemed to have an extra-close bond to Jesus.

John is the disciple who seemed to be a shadow at Jesus' side. When Jesus was hanging from the cross and saying goodbye to His earthly mother, Jesus asked John to care for her. The time John spent with Jesus had a profound impact on the disciple, and he became forever known by the love he shared with the Messiah.

In his writing and teaching, John could not stop mentioning the love of God. The mention of divine love saturates the gospel of John as well as 1, 2, and 3 John. Now this isn't the doe-eyed, infatuation kind of love you hear about in pop music or TV dating shows. The love John mentions is deep, passionate, and eternal. John discusses the kind of love every human soul craves. A love that satisfies our deepest needs. A love that beckons us toward God. A love that cannot be contained.

Of all the emotions God gives us, the greatest and most powerful is love.

John became so aware, captivated, and saturated by the love of God that it reshaped the core of who he was—his identity. Instead of referring to himself as "John" in the gospel he penned, John, also known as the beloved disciple, began referring to himself as the one "whom Jesus loved" (John 13:23; 19:26; 20:2; 21:7, 20).

The love John felt for and from Christ was so powerful that it consumed everything he said and did. The reality of God's love was so alive in his life that it shaped the way John saw others and especially himself. John wanted everyone to experience the same unconditional love that he felt on a moment-by-moment basis. And as his work appears throughout the New Testament, we are reminded that being loved by Christ and loving Christ affects the way we treat others. Casual observers will be able to tell we are followers of Jesus just by the love we have for each other. And the source of all this love is God Himself. Love is the essence of who God is. God *is* love.

Of all the emotions God gives us, the greatest and most powerful is love. When we wrap our emotions and ourselves in love, we find ourselves living life to the fullest and becoming a source of encouragement and inspiration to others. Love awakens in us a sense of adoration, fondness, compassion, tenderness, and longing, not just for God, but for others as God's love pours through us.

The more we get to know God, the more we partake of the fullness of love that has been shown to us through Christ, and the more filled with love we become. Eventually, that love fills our hearts to the brim, and it begins to overflow on all those around us. Like John, we become consumed with this amazing love—and it, in turn, becomes the foundation for our identity and everything we say, feel, think, and do.

1. *Describe a time in your life when you made sure to wrap your emotions in love before you responded to a situation. What was the result?*

2. *Describe a time in your life when you didn't wrap your emotions in love before you responded to someone. What was the result?*

3. *Why is it important to wrap yourself and your emotions in love? How does wrapping your emotions in love help you respond to others in healthy ways and prevent you from responding in hurtful ways?*

4. *Read* **1 John 4:6–12***. According to this passage, what is the source of love? How did God show love to us?*

A teacher of the law approached Jesus and wanted to know which commandment was the greatest. In reply, Jesus quoted a passage known as the *shema*—a Hebrew prayer recited frequently in Jewish prayer services.

5. *Read* **Matthew 22:36-40** *and* **Deuteronomy 6:4–9***. Why do you think Jesus chose to recite this passage in Luke 10?*

6. *We are called to love God with everything. Fill in the chart below according to* **Matthew 22:37**. *In the second column, write down how you can love God in that way.*

7. *What is the hardest part of loving others with your emotions?*

8. *How in the next week can you overflow with love for others?*

We are called to show God and others the greatest emotion of all: love!

Digging Deeper

Read **1 Corinthians 13:4–13**. On a blank sheet of paper, make a list of all the things that love is, as well as all the things that love is not. Next to each one, write down how you can more fully embody that aspect of pure, selfless love in your own life.

Bonus Activity

Write a love letter to God. Write down how thankful you are for Him and His love for you. Spend time praising God for His character. Keep the love note someplace where you can continue to add to it throughout the upcoming week.

Leader's Guide

Chapter 1: Rejoice! And Again I Say Rejoice!

***Focus:** The Psalms are a powerful reminder that we can bring our whole selves, including our emotions, before God, and discover God's loving care no matter what we're facing.*

1. *Use this icebreaker question to invite participants to discuss their own emotional responses to both challenges and delights in life. Because of life experiences, some people may have shifted the way they respond emotionally to situations and challenges. Encourage the group to discuss and share from their own lives.*

2. *Often our greatest strengths are connected to our greatest weaknesses. We may be an Emotional Responder, which gives us great empathy but also makes us less than objective. We may be a strong Thinking Responder but unable to naturally empathize with what others are feeling. We may be reserved and even-keeled, but unable to feel the emotional lighthearted delight that others experience.*

3. *Emotions include sadness, brokenness, pain, anguish, depression, exhaustion, hope, and comfort, among others.*

4. *Encourage participants to share a specific moment that their emotional response or perspective changed. If participants are slow to respond, offer an example from your own life to stir the discussion.*

5. *Answers will vary, but will probably include close family members and friends.*

6. *In the process of expressing our emotions and feelings and thoughts to God, we can be transformed in our attitude and perspective.*

7. *Answers will vary, but this is primarily a thanksgiving psalm expressing gratitude for God. Encourage participants to share stories of God's presence and faithfulness in their lives.*

8. *Fear of rejection or an unhealthy understanding of God-given emotions can prevent us from wholly expressing ourselves to God. The Psalms remind us that God welcomes us just as we are, but in His love He doesn't leave us there.*

Digging Deeper

Answers will vary, but we can find great encouragement and hope from studying the Psalms. We're reminded we're not alone in the challenges we're facing. God is with us. Through prayer and song, our perspective changes so we can once again celebrate the goodness and faithfulness of God.

Chapter 2: Spiritual Awakenings

Focus: *Spiritual awakenings in our lives rarely happen apart from our emotions. Most often when we encounter God we'll feel a sense of the joy, delight, confidence, or hope that comes from knowing God more intimately.*

1. *While many of our experiences are not as dramatic as the Wesley brothers', it's important to remember that God will often catch us by surprise in order to awaken our hearts to Him in an unexpected way.*

2. *The Wesley brothers' experiences can be called personal spiritual awakenings, moments when God awoke them to the reality of His presence and purpose for their lives. Some may argue that one can awake spiritually without an emotional response, but when we encounter God in a profound way, it's hard not be excited, joyful, and hopeful.*

3. *They probably felt discouraged and questioning, then encouraged and challenged and excited.*

4. *The men seemed honestly intrigued and hopeful that Jesus was the Messiah, but His death had taken them by surprise. They seemed to be reeling from all the reports coming in since Jesus' death.*

5. *Jesus rebuked them for being foolish and slow to believe. The rebuke was warranted or Jesus wouldn't have given it, and it's often true in our lives whenever we choose to believe a portion of what Jesus taught instead of everything.*

6. *The men urged Jesus to stay with them. They actually built a case as to why Jesus should stay—the day was ending, which implied it was not safe to travel at night. Sometimes we need to invite God to remain with us throughout the day through prayer or devotions or simply meditating on Him.*

7. *They may have felt a mixture of excitement, anticipation, joy, delight, hope, and expectation, among other emotions.*

8. *Encourage people to share specific stories of meaningful passages from their own lives. For those who have not experienced this feeling, encourage them to spend time in the Scriptures listening for what God might reveal to them and take note of how those experiences make them feel.*

Digging Deeper

Jeremiah described not speaking on behalf of God as burning fire shut up in his bones. He literally could not contain the fire, the passion, which he carried for God. As a prophet, Jeremiah was created to deliver the word of the Lord to the people, but that didn't mean the people responded well to what Jeremiah had to say.

Chapter 3: The Wonder of Divine Emotions

Focus: *Jesus displayed a wide range of emotions, and so do we. There is freedom in allowing ourselves to process those emotions. The challenge comes in handling our emotions in ways that reflect His work in our lives.*

1. *Answers will vary.*

2. *It reveals that even if Jesus had left immediately, Lazarus was already dead. Jesus knew this and also knew what was about to happen, making His mourning even more meaningful. The story reveals Jesus' deep love for His friends.*

3. *Jesus felt amazement toward the centurion. Some translations describe Jesus as marveling at the man. That's an incredible emotion to stir up in Jesus. As a result, the man's son was healed.*

4. *Jesus felt compassion for the woman who had lost her only son. Jesus touched the coffin and the man returned to life.*

5. *Jesus felt sternness. Jesus quieted the storm with His rebuke.*

6. *Jesus rejoiced and felt joy, happiness, and delight. He prayed to God a prayer of thanksgiving.*

7. *Consider times at home, with family, at work, or in your community.*

8. *Consider times at home, with family, at work, or in your community.*

Digging Deeper

The response to finding that which is lost is one of joy and rejoicing. Emotions may range from confidence to excitement to contentment to relief.

Chapter 4: Fear Not! Well, Maybe a Little!

Focus: *While we aren't meant to live in fear, a healthy dose of fear helps keep us safe, allows us to walk in wisdom, and provides an appropriate understanding of our limitations.*

1. *The fact that the mouse's fears didn't change despite his change of shape is surprising. One would think that a dog would no longer have the same heart as a mouse. Participants may relate in that they still have fears that have not subsided despite any changes they have made in their own lives.*

2. *Answers may include heights, spiders, snakes, being alone, and other responses. This question is designed for the participants to engage in a fun conversation about fears. As a leader, consider googling the top ten most common fears and share them with the group.*

3. *The disciples saw Jesus walking on water and were afraid because they thought He was a ghost. Jesus told them to "Take courage! It is I. Don't be afraid." Answers will vary, but often when our lives seem out of control, it is difficult and terrifying to remember that Jesus is in control.*

4. *Peter was walking on water and became scared of the wind. Jesus caught Peter and asked him why he doubted. Even if we have clear instructions from the Lord, it is still easy to find ourselves doubting.*

5. *This continuum is designed to get the participants thinking about how they react to Jesus calling them to action. Prayer, quoting Scripture, and the presence of other believers can help us to live more boldly.*

6. *Isaiah 11:2–3: has to do with knowledge*

   Proverbs 1:7: the beginning of knowledge

   Proverbs 9:10: the beginning of wisdom; insight

Proverbs 15:33: the instruction of wisdom

Psalm 130:3–4: because of God's forgiveness, He is feared

The fear of the Lord is often described in Scripture as the beginning of wisdom. "Fear" as it is used in these verses is sometimes misunderstood as synonymous with our common fears (heights, spiders, and so on), though in this case it is meant to describe awestruck reverence for God.

7. *A healthy fear of the Lord results in a genuine respect and delight in who God is. A healthy fear of the Lord recognizes our dependence on God and celebrates the attributes of God, including His holiness, wisdom, love, and grace.*

8. *There are countless ways to move away from a life defined by unhealthy fear, but prayer is always key. We can ask God to give us the courage and faith to move away from the fears that impede our lives and learn to live more holy lives.*

Digging Deeper

We are not meant to have a spirit of timidity. Instead, we are given a spirit of power, love, and self-discipline. Faith in God is the key to embracing and living out of this God-given spirit.

Chapter 5: A Healthy and Holy Dose of Anger

Focus: *While we may be tempted to dismiss anger as an emotion we'd rather not feel, anger can be a gift from God designed to awaken in us a desire for justice and caring for others.*

1. *Many times in our lives we encounter injustice that stirs up righteous anger—just like what happened with Shana. Traveling, watching the news, and even witnessing experiences in our own communities can stir that anger toward injustice.*

2. *Answers will vary, but could include feeling anger toward family, friends, or coworkers, while driving, or while waiting in line.*

3. *The people were being disobedient toward the commandments laid out in the Old Testament. This occurred during Passover—when Jews would pilgrimage to the temple. The people were turning the temple (God's house) into a market. They turned a house of worship into a place of commerce. Jesus cleared the merchants and their products out of the temple. He acted upon His anger in order to make things right. He worked on purifying the temple.*

4. *This outburst of anger would probably not be deemed appropriate behavior in our modern culture. A modern equivalent of Jesus' response may be like Shana's story in the intro—someone who stands up to fix the injustices she witnesses.*

5. *James 1:19–20: Be quick to listen and slow to become angry; anger does not produce righteousness.*

   Ephesians 4:26: Do not sin in anger and do not let the sun go down on your anger.

   Proverbs 14:29: Quick-tempered people display folly.

   Matthew 5:22–24: Make peace with your enemies before you can show honor to the Lord.

   Answers will vary. The participants may feel encouraged or challenged about each of these passages in various ways.

6. *Cain was angry and downcast because the Lord didn't look on his offering with favor, but did look at Abel's favorably. For some, tempers are easily ignited by bad drivers, a bad day, or a lack of customer service.*

7. *Cain was cursed and driven away to be a fugitive. The land would no longer yield crops for him, and he would be a restless wanderer. The Lord said He would hide His face from Cain—the worst punishment of all. Often when we sin out of our anger, we may feel distant from God.*

8. *Challenge participants to be more in tune with the differences between healthy, righteous anger and unhealthy anger that leads to sin.*

Digging Deeper

Jesus was indignant that the children had been kept from Him. He corrected the disciples then embraced the children. With this rebuke, Jesus was showing that He loves everyone and no one should be turned away from Him.

Chapter 6: The Unexpected Gift of Sadness

Focus: *On a list of emotions we try to avoid, sadness often tops the list! Yet not only is feeling sad normal, it's a gift from God. Sadness prompts us to pray, reminds us that we need others, calls us to honesty with ourselves and God, and creates compassion for others in our hearts.*

1. *The Lord viewed Job as a blameless and upright man who feared God and turned from evil. Satan criticized Job and said that the Lord had kept him protected. The Lord was still in control–He was the one who allowed Satan to ruin Job's life. God gave permission and set the boundaries for Satan's test.*

2. *Job lost all his servants, oxen, donkeys, sheep, camels, sons, and daughters. We would experience similar sadness and pain if we lost even some of what Job lost that day.*

3. *Job's wife wanted Job to curse the Lord and die. Job's friends sat with him without speaking.*

4. *Answers will vary among participants.*

5. *Job 1:20–22: He praised the name of the Lord.*

   Job 9:1–24: He praised God's transcendence and greatness.

   Job 13:15: He continued hoping in the Lord.

   Job 42:2: He accepted that God's plans cannot be altered or ruined.

6. Answers

Scripture	What God Asks Job	What Is Revealed about God
Job 38:4	Where were you when I laid the foundations of the earth?	God created the earth's foundation.
Job 38:8	Who shut in the sea with doors, when it burst forth and issued from the womb?	God has control over the seas.
Job 38:12	Have you commanded the morning since your days began, and caused the dawn to know its place?	God orders the morning and the sun.
Job 38:18	Have you comprehended the breadth of the earth?	God understands everything about the earth.
Job 38:19	Where is the way to the dwelling of light? And darkness, where is its place?	God understands light and darkness.
Job 38:22	Have you entered the treasury of snow, or have you seen the treasury of hail?	God created snow and hail.
Job 38:24–25	By what way is light diffused, or the east wind scattered over the earth? Who has divided a channel for the overflowing water, or a path for the thunderbolt?	God controls all weather.
Job 38:29	From whose womb comes the ice? And the frost of heaven, who gives it birth?	God controls ice and frost.
Job 38:32	Can you bring out Mazzaroth in its season? Or can you guide the Great Bear with its cubs?	The Lord commands the stars and the animals.
Job 38:36–37	Who has put wisdom in the mind? Or who has given understanding to the heart? Who can number the clouds by wisdom? Or who can pour out the bottles of heaven?	God created wisdom.
Job 38:41	Who provides food for the raven, when its young ones cry to God, and wander about for lack of food?	God cares and provides for His creation.

7. *Job learned that God is wiser than Job would ever be. Allow participants to share insights about God's character that they have learned through their own experiences.*

8. *Sometimes in our seasons of loss and pain, God chooses to reveal Himself to us in ways we couldn't imagine. It is through those trials we draw nearer to the Lord.*

Digging Deeper

Job's brothers, his sisters, and everyone who knew him came to Job's home exhibiting their kindness and support. They comforted and consoled Job by being with him, and they even gave him gifts. We, too, can offer our presence, encouragement, support, prayers, and gifts when people are going through and recovering from difficult times.

Chapter 7: A Holy Surprise

Focus: *Surprise may be one of the most delightful and unexpected gifts God gives us. God often surprises us and leaves us in awe of His mercy, compassion, kindness, and goodness.*

1. *Answers will vary.*

2. *We can get caught by surprise by unexpected guests stopping by, unexpected announcements or events from family members, surprise projects and deadlines, as well as unexpected curve balls life throws at us.*

3. Answers

Scripture	Who Was Surprised	The Surprise
Luke 1:9	Zechariah	Chosen by lot to enter the temple
Luke 1:11–12	Zechariah	An angel appeared
Luke 1:13–15	Zechariah	The angel said Zechariah's wife would have a son favored by God
Luke 1:20	Zechariah	Doubting the news, he was made mute
Luke 1:21–22	People	Zechariah's absence and muteness
Luke 1:24–25	Elizabeth	She became pregnant
Luke 1:28–29	Mary	An angel appeared
Luke 1:31	Mary	She would have a son favored by God
Luke 1:34–35	Mary	She would become pregnant as a virgin
Luke 1:41	Elizabeth	The baby responded to Mary's arrival and Elizabeth was filled with the Holy Spirit
Luke 1:63	Elizabeth and Zechariah	They had chosen the same baby name without discussing it
Luke 1:64–66	Everyone	Surprised at events

4. *God surprises people with His presence, faithfulness, and goodness, in order to show His vastness and to bring us into proper awe of His presence, actions, and involvement in our world.*

5. *Answers will vary.*

6. *The surprise is available in both—God works in the big picture as well as the minutest details.*

7. *When we declare the kindness of the Lord, we can't help but praise Him for His goodness and share it with others.*

8. *Through prayer, we can ask God to surprise us. That's a prayer that God probably won't say no to! We can also be more intentional about looking at the small ways God is moving and working in our lives and the lives of those around us and celebrate His presence.*

Digging Deeper

Everyone was probably surprised—Peter who was awoken by an angel, Rhoda who was so excited by the surprise she left Peter, the people who couldn't believe the answer to prayer and release of Peter.

Chapter 8: Contagious Joy

Focus: *The Lord desires to be the source of the joy and hope that strengthens us regardless of our circumstances.*

1. *Everyone has been around people who exude the joy of Christ. They are optimistic and positive, kind, and seemingly full of peace. Just being around them makes you feel more hopeful and encouraged in your own faith. Joyful people often make choices to focus on the positive, trust God, and not get caught up in things that will pull them down.*

2. *Joy is contagious, and everyone has had a joyful person rub off on them at one time or another.*

3. *Unfortunately, the contagious aspect of attitude is conversely true. Negativity breeds negativity. Encourage the group to share ideas about how to handle a truly negative situation in a way that honors God without dishonoring the person.*

4. *Answers*

Scripture	Insight on Joy
Psalm 16:11	The Lord's presence can fill us with joy.
Psalm 5:11	All who take refuge in the Lord will sing for joy.
Psalm 33:1	We should sing joyful praises to the Lord.
Psalm 90:14	The Lord's mercy gives us reason to rejoice and be glad.
1 Chronicles 16:27	Joy is in the Lord's dwelling place; it is part of His essence.
Zephaniah 3:17	The Lord loves us and rejoices over us with singing.
Galatians 5:22–23	Joy is a fruit of the spirit working in our lives.

5. *Encourage participants to look inward and see that their outlook and attitude can affect those around them. Have them look honestly at their lives and allow the Holy Spirit to change anything that may need attention.*

6. *Answers will vary.*

7. *The apostles may have considered giving up, but the joy of the Lord was their strength and gave them the hope and encouragement they needed to keep moving forward in obedience. The amazing thing about joy is that it does not depend on circumstances or other people. It finds its only base in the Lord, who is never changing.*

8. *Areas of work, family, day-to-day activities, and relationships may be common answers to this question.*

Digging Deeper

Answers will vary, but there is a direct correlation between our love for God and obedience. With great love and obedience comes great joy directly to our hearts from Jesus.

Chapter 9: The Wonders of the Calm

Focus: *We can find comfort in God. No matter what storms of life we're experiencing, God wants to give us a sense of His calmness.*

1. *This question is designed to spark fun, lighthearted conversation for the group icebreaker.*

2. *Often, we find that our pets can teach us a lot about life and about God's character. Have participants share a time in their own lives where their pet has enlightened them to a principle or truth about God.*

3. *Often it becomes easy for us to distance our lives from God– thinking that He could never understand the pain or hurt or fear we experience. However, we need to be reminded that God has power over everything. Knowing that He is in control can be a great comfort.*

4. *Answers*

What Was Formed		What It Was Filled With	
Day 1:	Day and night	Day 4:	Sun, moon, stars
Day 2:	Sky and water	Day 5:	Birds and fish
Day 3:	Land and seas (vegetation)	Day 6:	Living creatures and man

God purposely designed the days in a specific order. Days 1, 2, and 3 create the space that is filled by what was created on days 4, 5, and 6.

5. *Jesus offers rest for the weak and weary. He offers comfort for the burdened. We all have experienced overload and heavy burdens. But Jesus offers to remove those and give us rest.*

6. *Often in our weakness, we can become so overwhelmed we don't even know where to start in prayer. Paul promised us in Romans that in these situations, the Spirit knows our wordless groans and speaks on our behalf.*

7. *Knowing we have God on our side–desiring intimacy and offering us comfort–can fill us with confidence when we find ourselves confronted by weaknesses. Even when we are most afraid or feel the most alone, we can be sure that we have the highest of all powers on our side.*

8. *By not leaning on ourselves to find comfort and relief from daily stresses, we are more fully able to rely on God to sustain us and give us calm. Challenge participants to dive into Scripture and prayer when they feel a need for comfort from the Creator.*

Digging Deeper

The psalmist used the illustration of God as a bird. Seeking God as our shelter means going to Him in times of trouble, stress, fear, and abandonment.

Chapter 10: Growing in Trust

***Focus:** God invites us to place our trust in Him. When we trust in God, we will never be abandoned or disappointed.*

1. *Gently encourage honest sharing to this difficult question.*

2. *Gently encourage honest sharing to this question. Lack of trust can drive a wedge between people, fuel miscommunication, and destroy intimacy.*

4. *The psalmist had his trust in the goodness of people and life shattered. He watched as the wicked prospered, as they spoke cruel words and lived as if they were God. The psalmist described himself as being afflicted every day with new punishments every morning (v. 14). Whether these abuses were emotional, physical, or something else, we do not know. But we do know the psalmist's grieved and embittered heart was changed by God.*

5. *Answers will vary but may include God, prayer, and people who have been a source of healing and encouragement.*

6. *Answers*

Scripture	Reveals about Trust	True in Your Life
Proverbs 30:5	Every word of the Lord is flawless; He protects those who trust Him.	Answers will vary. Encourage participants to share how they have found these passages to be true in their own lives.
2 Samuel 22:31	The word of the Lord is flawless and has proven trustworthy.	
Psalm 36:7	God's love is unfailing and all people find refuge in His wings.	
Psalm 118:8	It is better to take refuge in the Lord than trust in man.	

7. *We may be tempted to place our trust in people who at some point will disappoint us. We may be tempted to place our trust or security in money, wealth, position, power, or proximity, but all of these are fading and changing. God alone is who we can trust.*

8. *Answers will vary, but when we don't pray or take time to consult God with our lives, we are left to our devices to make decisions. The passage invites participants to reflect on how God wants us to trust Him with everything all the time. Steps for change may include praying, studying the Scripture, spending time with a Christian counselor, confessing sins, and taking time to talk to God honestly about the past.*

Digging Deeper

The author of this psalm warned against placing one's trust in human beings. Because of the fallen nature of humans, we often let each other down. We all have experienced times when our trust has been broken in human relationships. Instead, the psalmist said that those who place their trust in the Lord are blessed.

Chapter 11: Hopeful and Hope-Filled

Focus: *Hope is an essential emotion—one we can't live without. When we combine hope with faith, we find ourselves joyfully trusting God with everything.*

1. *This question is designed to get participants to share stories from their own journeys of seeing people whose stories are marked by hope.*

2. *The woman had suffered from bleeding for twelve years. After having spent all her money seeing numerous doctors, none had been able to help her. In fact, she had only gotten worse.*

3. *The woman would have been considered unclean. Anything she sat on or lay in would be considered unclean. Anyone who touched her would be considered unclean. She was considered an outcast—completely rejected by society because of her illness. This probably left the woman hopeless, alone, and discouraged.*

4. *Jesus healed her and freed her from her suffering.*

5. *Jairus pleaded with Jesus to save his daughter. He also knew his daughter could be healed simply by the touch of the Lord. The difference is that the woman did not ask Jesus for healing; she just touched His cloak. Jairus's daughter died, but Jesus still healed her. When we place our hope in Jesus, He is faithful no matter what the situation.*

6. Answers

Scripture	Blessings and Rewards of Hope	Your Experience
Psalm 31:24	Strength and courage	Answers will vary, but encourage participants to think about times where they have experienced these rewards because of hoping in the Lord.
Psalm 33:18	Protection	
Psalm 146:5	Blessing or happiness	
Proverbs 10:28	Gladness	
1 Thessalonians 4:13	Comfort	

7. *Often we want to take matters into our own hands rather than trust in the unseen. Sometimes we feel that God works too slowly or not obviously enough. Gently encourage participants to share their feelings and experiences on this topic.*

8. *Encourage participants to hold each other accountable as they learn to place their hope in the Lord.*

Digging Deeper

Paul described God as the God of hope. While our own experiences of this may vary, continually throughout Scripture we can see men and women who placed their hope in the Lord and were blessed and rewarded. The source of our hope is the Holy Spirit. By overflowing with hope in the Lord, we will be filled with His blessings. Encourage participants to share stories of their hope-filled week at the next session.

Chapter 12 Abounding in Love

Focus: ***We are called to show God and others the greatest emotion of all: love!***

1. *Use this question to spur conversation around the importance of making sure our emotions are wrapped in love before we respond to others.*

2. *Use this question to spur conversation around the importance of making sure our emotions are wrapped in love before we respond to others.*

3. *Without love, we may be tempted to allow our emotions to get the best of us and respond in hurtful and harmful ways that undermine our relationships.*

4. *God is the source of our love. God showed His love to us through His Son, Jesus.*

5. *Jesus knew the significance of this passage to Jews—especially this teacher of the law. The teacher of the law attempted to trip Jesus up and find fault in His theology, but Jesus proved that He proclaimed the God of Israel also.*

6. *Answers*

Love the Lord Your God with All Your . . .	How I Can Love God That Way
Heart	Ex: I can do everything to love God with my emotional self.
Soul	I can do everything to love God with my spiritual being.
Strength	I can do everything in my power to love God with my strength–with my physical being.
Mind	I can do everything in my power to love God with my mind.

7. *We are called to love one another. Oftentimes, loving others is difficult, but when we know and experience the love of God, we are able to overflow with love for others.*

8. *Encourage participants to think of practical ways they can express the love of God in their own lives this week.*

Digging Deeper

Love is patient, kind, keeps no record of wrongs, truthful, protecting, trusting, hopeful, persevering. Love is not envious, boastful, proud, self-seeking, dishonoring, easily angered, evil.

Notes

Chapter 2

1. http://www.ccel.org/ccel/wesley/journal.vi.xii.xxii.html.

Chapter 8

1. http://www.physorg.com/news198250962.html; http://news.bbc.co.uk/2/hi/health/2158336.stm; http://www.umm.edu/news/releases/laughter2.htm.
2. http://latimesblogs.latimes.com/booster_shots/2010/07/how-are-sadness-and-happiness-like-diseases-theyre-infectious-study-finds.html.

Chapter 9

1. Marilee Parrish, "A Hiding Place," *Heavenly Humor for the Dog Lover's Soul* (Uhrichsville, OH: Barbour Publishing, 2010), 157–58.

Chapter 11

1. http://news.bbc.co.uk/2/hi/8257153.stm.

About the Author

A popular speaker at churches and leading conferences such as Catalyst and Thrive, Margaret Feinberg was recently named one of the "30 Voices" who will help lead the church in the next decade by *Charisma* magazine. She has written more than two dozen books and Bible studies, including the critically acclaimed *The Organic God*, *The Sacred Echo*, *Scouting the Divine*, and their corresponding DVD Bible studies. She is known for her relational teaching style and inviting people to discover the relevance of God and His Word in a modern world.

Margaret and her books have been covered by national media, including: CNN, the Associated Press, *Los Angeles Times*, Dallas Morning News, *Washington Post*, *Chicago Tribune*, and many others. She currently lives in Colorado, with her 6'8" husband, Leif, and superpup, Hershey. Go ahead, become her friend on Facebook, follow her on Twitter @mafeinberg, add her on Google+ or check out her website at www.margaretfeinberg.com.